The word "essay" derives from the   t." For
hundreds of years, writers have used the term as an attempt to understand philosophical
questions and to teach their readers. Today, the essay is everywhere. Articles in
newspapers and magazines are non-academic essays. Famous essayists have written on
every subject, from literature and philosophy to the history of ice cream, baseball and
politics. People read essays as much for the pleasure they might get from a short story or
a novel as for the opportunity to learn about new subjects.

Even if in the weeks to come we will use the essay to discuss history and literature, you
should remember that it can just as easily be used to analyze your dog's behavior or your
own. In fact, trying to understand oneself has preoccupied many essay writers. Almost
every great thinker in recent history wrote essays in order to share his ideas with the
world.

Facts about the essay:

- The first author to describe his works as essays was Michel de Montaigne (1533-1592). Inspired by the Greek biographer Plutarch (46-120), he began to compose his essays in 1572.
- The first Englishman to call his writing "essays" was Francis Bacon (1561-1626).
- In 1609, according to the Oxford English Dictionary, the English dramatist and poet Ben Jonson first used the word "essayist."

Famous Essayists:

Michel de Montaigne
Francis Bacon
Virginia Woolf
Voltaire
Joan Didion
Susan Sontag
Annie Dillard
Leo Tolstoy
Aldous Huxley
Anne Fadiman
William Hazlitt
Ralph Waldo Emerson
Henry David Thoreau
George Orwell
George Bernard Shaw
Marguerite Yourcenar
E.B. White
J.M. Coetzee

The Three Parts: the Five-Paragraph Essay

Though not all essays need to have three main parts, the basic essay is called the "five paragraph essay," sometimes referred to as the "three-five essay." It has *five* paragraphs in all: *three* main body paragraphs, an introduction and a conclusion.

Though this essay form developed over hundreds of years, we still use it today because of its basic principles. It developed as both a *rational* and a *legal* form. Sound complicated? It's actually fairly simple.

The Rational Form of the Essay

Let's look at the essay from a *rational* standpoint.

Introduction: asks a question.
>   Is war necessary?

Body paragraph 1: offers one viewpoint.
>   Explains why war is necessary.

Body paragraph 2: offers the opposite viewpoint.
>   Explains why war is not necessary.

Body paragraph 3: examines which viewpoint is best.
>   Since so few societies have lived without war, war appears
>   necessary, but not ideal.

Conclusion: sums up the argument and discusses loose ends and future questions.
>   Little proof exists that societies can live without war; however, a
>   lack of evidence does not necessarily prove an argument.
>   Moreover, could the suffering caused by war be an argument in
>   itself against war?

Rational Essay Practice

Imagine two possible topics for the rational form.
Usually they are in the form of questions.

Here are a couple if you're feeling stuck:

1. Does TV fry your brain?

2. Is it OK to download files from the Internet even if it is a violation of copyright law?

Pick the one that interests you the most.

Now fill in the sections below.
If you get confused, refer back to the example on the previous page.

Introduction: asks your question.

Body paragraph 1: offers one viewpoint.

Body paragraph 2: offers the opposite viewpoint.

Body paragraph 3: examines which viewpoint is best.

Conclusion: gives a summation of the argument and discusses loose ends and future questions.

The Legal Form of the Essay

Now let's look at it from a *legal* standpoint (in fact, the essay has existed as a legal form for over nine hundred years). This time you are a lawyer, and you have to prove the innocence of your client, Mr. Clovis, who is in court for stealing vegetables from a neighbor's garden.

Introduction: you introduce Mr. Clovis to the court and tell us a bit about him. He's a responsible man, has three children and has never missed a day of work in his life. However, our good citizen Mr. Clovis is now on trial for having stolen thirteen carrots from the garden of his neighbor, Mr. Panikos, a Greek immigrant who is also a very respected member of the town.

Body paragraph 1: Explain why Mr. Clovis should be considered innocent. He has never done anything wrong before and why would he start off a career in crime by carrot theft. Bring in a witness who claims he is innocent. Then end the paragraph with the strongest evidence yet. The carrots were found on the front porch and most likely were torn up and left there by a prankster.

Body paragraph 2: Here we have the evidence against Mr. Clovis. New witnesses take the stand and they claim that they saw him in the garden, or that they noticed him eyeing the carrots greedily, or that he particularly loved carrot soup.

Body paragraph 3: We compare the evidence, examine the contradictions and highlight the similarities. If this were a crime novel or a trial movie, you, as the writer, would be at your best, making stunning comparisons, analyzing the testimonies.

Conclusion: You, the lawyer, stand before the jury or the judge. You give your summary of all that has happened though now you deliver your information a little differently. Even though you repeat many things from the previous paragraphs, you give them a slant intended to make us agree with one side. In a perfect world, you would repeat the information in such a way as to convince us of the innocence of the person who really is innocent.

Legal Essay Practice

Practice: Sketch out one of the two following *legal* essays or come up with your own idea. Imagine your supporting information, what your witnesses might say.

Remember that when you are writing this, you are the lawyer.

1. Mary Lawson has accused Joseph Pellerino of cheating during a math exam. Using students testimonies, present a sketch of this case.

2. Mr. Wilson's wife, Mrs. Wilson, has accused him of selling top secret government plans to a group of extraterrestrials who meet him on the roof each Wednesday night.

Fill in the information below:

Introduction (introduce your client): his situation, personality and the accusations leveled against him.

Body Paragraph 1: Why is he innocent? Who are your witnesses?

Body Paragraph 2: What might he be guilty? Who is there witness against him?

Body Paragraph 3: Compare the two arguments and show why yours is best.

Conclusion: Face the jury. Remember that they haven't entirely decided yet. Now you have to rephrase your information so that it sounds concise and convincing. Don't forget to dismiss any lingering doubts they might have.

The Five-Paragraph Essay Today

While the five paragraph essay remains quite popular today, the compare and contrast structure is no longer the primary approach. The form has been adapted in favor of developmental essays in which each of the three paragraphs develops a different aspect of the main question. For instance, what do the three colors of the French flag symbolize, or what are three characteristics that distinguish a whale from a shark? In truth, developmental or expository essays can have more than three body paragraphs, but for the purpose of a developing a strong essay-writing technique, it is best to work with shorter essays.

What's best? Long or short essays?

The seventeenth century French philosopher Blaise Pascal wrote in a letter: "*I have made this letter rather long only because I have not had time to make it shorter.*" This quotation became famous because of how clearly it showed the truth about writing. Often, students sit down with a stack of research and transform it into a long, sprawling paper filled with details. When they turn it in, they tend to feel proud of having written such a long essay; however, when their teacher gets it and starts reading, he often thinks, "Oh no, so much information without organization or clear ideas." You've nearly drowned him in details, but *why* did you choose those particular details? He doesn't know. He wishes for a crisp, powerful *short* essay.

An essayist who knows his material through and through can convey it much more *succinctly* and quickly than can an essayist who hasn't processed and internalized the information. Brevity is like wit. You have to have come up with a clear idea that you can deliver quickly. A one-liner is almost always more powerful than a long-winded reply.

For all these reasons, teachers often prefer that students start by writing shorter essays. This doesn't mean that you can have a one sentence paragraph! A two to four page essay is a good place to start. You begin by thinking about the research you've gathered. You analyze it and come up with your own ideas. Then you organize your ideas, and only once you know how your ideas fit together, do you bring back the *supporting* evidence.

The Types of Essays:

There are many types of essays: expository, persuasive, literary, compare and contrast, informal, analytical, research, narrative, descriptive, cause and effect, process.

More often than not the types of essays overlap. For instance, a literary essay about a novel can also be persuasive. It can try to convince its readers of one way of interpreting the story versus another. A literary essay can also be a compare and contrast essay, discussing the differences between two characters.

We will present each type of essay as we go.

The Expository Essay

The first essay that everyone learns is the *expository* essay, which is frequently referred to as a research report.

The word expository originally comes from Latin *expositor*, which means "one who exposes." The purpose of an expository essay is to inform, explain, describe, or define a subject to the reader, and therefore to 'expose' information. The expository essay is the most frequently used type of writing by students in high schools and universities. A well-written expository essay stays focused on its topic and gives facts in order to *inform* its reader. It should be unbiased and accurate.

Now that we've given you a brief overview of the essay and of the *expository* essay, let's proceed to the *introduction*.

The Art of the Introduction

In many ways, the introduction is the most important part of the essay. It prepares the reader, letting him know how he should make sense of the information that he will receive. Often times, even if the body of the essay isn't as strong, a great introduction will help the reader to understand what follows.

But introductions are also the place where an essayist shows her style. Sometimes the introduction is considered an essayist's signature. For instance, in your first sentence, you can try a stylish turn of phrase. Halfway through the essay, this is much more difficult because the reader has a lot of information to absorb and you don't want to lose his attention. But in the beginning, the reader is fresh and wants to be hooked in. With a good introduction, you can tell him not only how you're going to write but whether the subject interests him. A great essayist can make almost any subject sound interesting.

In this section, you will learn to give your introduction punch, momentum and purpose. Think of a novel or a movie. If the beginning is boring and hard to understand, do you really care what comes next?

Practice:
List two subjects or things that you consider incredibly boring.
(Some people think that the ballet and the symphony are boring while others can't stand to watch baseball on television. What are some things that put you right to sleep?

1.

2.

Now rewrite them to make them sound as exciting as possible.
Don't forget that the best way to do this is to read a bit about the subject and to use details.
Don't just make up something crazy about the subject.
Examine it.
Find what makes it interesting.

1.

2.

Part I
Knowing your essay's purpose: the thesis

Though the thesis is usually the last or second to last sentence in an introduction, it is the most important, and the rest of the introduction can't even be imagined without it. Trying to start an essay without knowing what you are writing about would be like packing your bags and going to the airport even though you have no ticket and no idea where you will be traveling. You wouldn't even know what to pack much less what to do once you arrived at the airport. You can consider the thesis as your ticket because most teachers won't let you write your essay until you have one, and a strong thesis is often a "ticket" to a good grade.

So what exactly is a thesis?

Hint: Look up "thesis" in the dictionary.

Some stuffy French academics like to sniff and talk about "*la problématique*" in an essay. This is often just a fancy way of saying thesis. They call it a problem because it still has to be proven. Unfortunately, this makes it all sound much more complicated than it really is.

A thesis is actually much simpler.
Consider the following scenarios:

1. You are walking home with a friend, and he claims to be a better student than you. As soon as you decide to prove him wrong, you are formulating a thesis. If you say, "You're wrong because I'm better at math, science and history," you've stated a thesis that you will go on to prove by referring not only to your grades but to your interest in the subjects you mentioned.

2. Rather than wanting to argue about intelligence, your friend sees a salamander on the sidewalk and says, "Look! A lizard!" While this could be proof for why you're better at science, it can also provide the inspiration for a new thesis. First, you reply, "Actually, it's a salamander." When he says, "Salamander, lizard, same thing!" then you deliver your thesis: "Lizards are reptiles which evolved from amphibians like the salamander, but their skin, the way they breathe, and their means of reproduction are quite different." Okay, maybe you wouldn't say it *exactly* like that, but if you did it would provide an excellent thesis.

The Thesis in Everyday Life

The truth is that we use some form of thesis every day even though we don't always get around to proving our *theses*.

Here's a possible list of poorly developed theses, followed by examples of how they could be developed as the subject matter of an essay:

– 1 –

Version 1. "You shouldn't blame me for eating the candy because I don't even like candy!"

Version 2. "Though unfairly accused of having eaten the candy, I am in truth innocent because not only do I dislike candy but I am allergic to sugar and I am terrified of cavities."

– 2 –

Version 1. "It's not my fault that I didn't do my homework."

Version 2. "Though homework can often be considered a student's responsibility, my failure to deliver today's homework is not my fault but rather the result of the following complications: a total absence of pens in my house, a dog that loves to eat paper of all sorts, and a loss of memory resulting from my extremely tight baseball cap."

– 3 –

Version 1. "He started it! I didn't do anything!"

Version 2. "We can objectively agree that he started the disagreement in question and that I did nothing wrong because he is cruel by nature and I, on the other hand, was asleep at the time and have a meek and gentle personality.

– 4 –

Version 1. "It's not fair!"

Version 2. "As wise men and children have stated throughout the ages, life is far from fair because the truth can be hard to find, good people don't always get heard, and, unlike in the fairy tales, the bad guy sometimes wins."

Practicing the Thesis in Everyday Life

Practice 1:

Write down something you might say when you get in an argument, and then try to rewrite it as eloquently as possible in the form of a thesis statement. In each thesis statement, include at least three reasons why you are right.

What you say in arguments:

Rewrite what you say in thesis form (don't forget to include three reasons why you're right:

Practice 2:

Write down a sentence that states something you believe firmly. Then try to transform it into a thesis. For example, "Be kind to other people" can become "It is wise to be kind to others because then you will have a good reputation, feel positive about yourself, and mostly likely be treated kindly in return."

Something that you believe to be true:

The idea rewritten as a thesis (don't forget to include the three main reasons):

The Expository Thesis Statement

Up to this point, we've mostly considered theses that prove an argument, but not every thesis needs to prove something. Often, it simply informs, as in an *expository* essay. Of course, even the most straightforward expository essay can sound as if it is persuading you of something. But this is because we often confuse teaching with persuading. A true persuasive essay has to convince you of its point and state both why we should believe something as well as why we should not. A *legal* essay tends to be persuasive whereas an *expository* essay tends to lay out the facts in such a way as to teach us something new.

The thesis of an *expository* essay should tell us a general topic as well as three things that we are going to learn about that topic. Consider it this way. Your job is to identify a general theme or topic regarding a person's life, and then to expose three aspects of that theme.

The three aspects of that theme should be listed in order of importance, starting with the least important and progressing to the most. The list can also be given chronologically in terms of years or process (for instance, explaining how a situation developed).

Practice: (To be completed as homework)
List two subjects about which you would like to know more.

1.

2.

Now think of three aspects that make each subject interesting.
(Look in the encyclopedia if necessary.)

1.
    a.

    b.

    c.

2.
    a.

    b.

    c.

Einstein: Examples of Expository Thesis Statements

In order to understand the thesis more clearly, let us turn our attention to one of the great geniuses of the twentieth century: *Einstein*.

Here are four expository thesis statements about Einstein. Read each one carefully.

1. At the core of Einstein's rebellious genius was his nonconformity, his questioning of accepted truths, and his strength to stand by what he believed even when others considered him a failure.

(This would be an essay explaining three aspects of his life that made him a rebellious genius.)

2. Einstein's belief that creativity cannot exist without a questioning of authority can be clearly seen during his high school and university studies, the time he spent working as a patent clerk, and even his years as world-famous celebrity.

(This essay would discuss the phases of his life and how during each phase he rejected authority.)

3. Though many of Einstein's greatest achievements took years to receive recognition, the source of his genius could already be seen in his youthful rebelliousness, his courage to take risks and his powerful imagination.

(This essay would examine three aspects of Einstein's youth that led to his being a genius.)

4. Though Einstein studied traditional physics, his genius grew from what others considered to be his failures: his problems in school, his inability to find a teaching position and his job as a patent clerk.

(This essay would show how each "failure" actually helped him in some way towards his goals.)

Practice 1:
1. Each thesis statement contains the three elements that will be the main topics for each of the essay's three body paragraphs. Go back and re-read each thesis statement. Highlight and number the three elements.

2. Again re-read each thesis and rewrite it in your own words. Highlight and number the three elements.

Practice: Think Different

Choose and highlight a historical figure from the list below.

Martin Luther King   Bob Dylan
Richard Branson   John Lennon and Yoko Ono
Buckminster Fuller   Thomas Alva Edison
Muhammad Ali   Ted Turner
Maria Callas   Gandhi
Amelia Earhart   Alfred Hitchcock
Martha Graham   Jim Henson
Frank Lloyd Wright   Pablo Picasso

- Now brainstorm attributes of your historical figure.
- Write out each attribute in no more than three words.

- Choose the attribute that you think is most important to your historical figure.
- This should be what makes him or her tick, or made him great. Write it below.
- Now brainstorm what events or circumstances gave him or her this quality.

- Pick three of the events or circumstances.
- Now write a thesis sentence for your historical figure.
- The main part of the thesis should be what makes him or her a genius
- The three supporting points or elements should be the events or circumstances.

- Highlight each of the three main points or elements and number them.

Part II
The first sentence: the hook

In the first sentences of an essay, a lecture or even a conversation, you, the writer or speaker, have your best opportunity to impress and hook your audience. This "first impression" is as important for essay writing as it is when meeting someone new or when doing a high school admissions interview. If the first word out of your mouth is, "Um..." the listener is still waiting for you to say something interesting. Essay writing has its own equivalent of "Um."

The *Um...* in essay writing: the *Platitude* (cliché, obvious statement).

Look up "Platitude" (when you look something up, the definition is more likely to stick).

For instance, if you are writing an essay about the genius of Einstein, you should not begin with the following:

Many intelligent people have changed the world.
or
Geniuses are rare and generally disliked, but their passion transforms society.
or
To be a genius is not easy, but in the end it is worth it.

What do these sentences specifically say about Einstein? Nothing. Rather, they repeat truisms, or platitudes, about the nature of genius. They could have been said about hundreds of other people, and for that reason you are no closer to telling your reader what makes Einstein so special.

So how do you make the very best use of your first sentence? You *hook* the reader or listener. Every now and then we hear someone speak, and we think to ourselves, 'I have to stick around for what she's going to say next.' When this happens, it is usually because the person has said something unexpected or informative, something that you hadn't previously known or imagined. An untrained ear might be impressed by a platitude, but platitudes are essentially empty chatter. Train your ear so that you can identify when someone is conveying actual information and not just repeating what everyone already knows.

In essay writing, a strong first sentence is called a *hook*. Sometimes known as "the lead" or "the motivator," the *hook* is a better term because we can visualize it. After the thesis statement, a good hook is the most challenging sentence to write in an essay.

Types of Hooks

A hook conveys specific and highly relevant information about the subject of the essay, in this case, Einstein. Don't forget that a reader, when he picks up your essay, hopes to find your subject inspiring. So whereas you don't have to be as brilliant as Einstein (at least not yet), you should try to capture a glimmer of his brilliance in your writing. The best way to do this in a hook is to give one of the following.

1. **Historical information**
2. **Character sketch**
3. **Anecdote**
4. **Surprising statement**
5. **Declaration**

These categories are not exclusive. For instance, a character sketch can be a surprising statement and include historical information. An anecdote can offer a character sketch as well as historical information. All of the first four generally work well with different types of essays (expository, persuasive, literary, research, etc.). However, number 5, the declaration, is generally best used when the essay has an element of persuasion.

Sample Hooks

1. Historical information

Not until 1919, fourteen years after Einstein wrote his ground-breaking scientific papers while working as a patent clerk, did the general public accept his predictions regarding the nature of light.

(This *historical information* is also an *anecdote* as well as a *surprising statement*.)

2. Character sketch (two versions)

In order to give himself the liberty necessary for creative thought, Einstein based his life on a firm rejection of authority and accepted that others would consider him a failure.

From his early teens on, Einstein's rejection of authority and admiration of creative thought gave him clarity not only in his scientific work but also in his political views.

(A *character sketch*, especially in the case of a historical figure, will usually give *historical information*.)

3. Anecdote

At the age of sixteen, the same year that Einstein dropped out of high school and failed the entrance examination to the Swiss Federal Institute of Technology, he also performed the famous thought experiment in which he visualized traveling alongside a beam of light.

(This *anecdote* is also *historical information* and even a *surprising statement*.)

4. Surprising statement

Though many considered Einstein's years working in the Swiss Patent Office to be a waste of his talent, he later claimed that the job gave him the creative space and even the inspiration for many of the ideas that he would later develop.

(Inevitably, this statement also provides *historical information*.)

5. Declaration

Were it not for Einstein's rejection of authority and his willingness to be seen as a failure, he would have lacked the creative space and intellectual detachment necessary to develop the Special Theory of Relativity.

(This is also a *surprising statement*; however, this declaration implies that the essay to follow will persuade us regarding the importance of Einstein's rebelliousness. We also expect that this essay's thesis statement will be an elaboration or a precision on this topic, or, at very least, related thematically.)

Do you now see the difference between a *hook* and a *platitude*? Go back and compare the two. The hook establishes the main idea of the essay as well as the tone and style that you will continue to develop all the way through to the conclusion. When you are telling your friends a story or attempting to convince them of an idea, try starting with a hook and then see what happens. After all, the best storytellers and the best debaters are often excellent essayists.

Practice 1:
Go back and re-read each hook several times and then rewrite it in your own words. Really try to understand what makes a hook powerful. After you have written each one, write one to two sentences for each hook, explaining why the hook is or is not powerful and why it would or world not hook your attention. For any hook that you think is not effective enough, explain what would make it stronger.

Practice 2:
Write four of the five types of hooks. Use the same historical figure you used for your thesis.

Martin Luther King	Bob Dylan
Richard Branson	John Lennon and Yoko Ono
Buckminster Fuller	Thomas Alva Edison
Muhammad Ali	Ted Turner
Maria Callas	Gandhi
Amelia Earhart	Alfred Hitchcock
Martha Graham	Jim Henson
Frank Lloyd Wright	Pablo Picasso

Practice: Pairing Hooks with Theses

Here is a series of hooks and theses that we've discussed. Try to decide which hook best fits with which thesis statement. This is a challenging project, and you might discover that there is more than one solution. Once you have chosen your pairs, write one to two sentences for each pair explaining why they fit together. Do you see in what ways the hook sets up the thesis? How might they work better together?

Hooks:

1. Not until 1919, fourteen years after Einstein wrote his ground-breaking scientific papers while working as a patent clerk, did the general public accept his predictions regarding the nature of light.

2. In order to give himself the liberty necessary for creative thought, Einstein based his life on a firm rejection of authority and accepted that others would consider him a failure.

3. At the age of sixteen, the same year that Einstein dropped out of high school and failed the entrance examination to the Swiss Federal Institute of Technology, he also performed the famous thought experiment in which he visualized traveling alongside a beam of light.

4. Though many considered Einstein's years working in the Swiss Patent Office to be a waste of his talent, he later claimed that the job gave him the creative space and even the inspiration for many of the ideas that he would later develop.

Thesis Statements:

1. At the core of Einstein's rebellious genius was his nonconformity, his questioning of accepted truths, and his strength to stand by what he believed even when others considered him a failure.

2. Einstein's belief that creativity cannot exist without a questioning of authority can be clearly seen during his high school and university studies, the time he spent working as a patent clerk, and even his years as world-famous celebrity.

3. Though many of Einstein's greatest achievements took years to receive recognition, the source of his genius could already be seen in his youthful rebelliousness, his courage to take risks and his powerful imagination.

4. Though Einstein studied traditional physics, his genius grew from what others considered to be his failures: his problems in school, his inability to find a teaching position and his job as a patent clerk.

Part III
Putting it all together: writing the context

With the hook and the thesis, you have found a way both to get our attention and to tell us what you're going to teach us. But how do you tie the two together? This is the introduction's *context*, the information that casually leads us from the hook to the thesis.

In the introduction, the context is the basic information that your reader needs in order to understand your thesis. The context can be the two *or more* sentences that link the hook and the thesis. While the *hook* catches out attention, the context connects it to the thesis, linking the two together.

Like the other elements of a good introduction, the context also requires control and planning. The danger is that you tell too much and steal from the body of your essay. In the introduction to a novel or a short story, writers offer hints about what is to come, but they make sure not to give their surprises away. An essay is no different.

Context Don'ts
- Don't tell too much.
- Don't start your analysis.
- Don't try to answer your thesis.
- Don't repeat your thesis or offer another thesis.
- Don't give information that belongs in the body paragraphs.

Context Dos
- Do give background information, such as historical events and dates.
- Do explain why the thesis question is important (if you can do so briefly).
- Do mention your primary subject (book or author or historical figure you are studying)
- Do offer supporting information for your thesis, but only if it is simple.

Bridging the *Hook* and the *Thesis*

For instance, let's connect one of the hooks and one of the theses that we've already seen.

The *context* is in *italics*.

Not until 1919, fourteen years after Einstein wrote his ground-breaking scientific papers while working as a patent clerk, did the general public accept his predictions regarding the nature of light. *However, what remains remarkable about his character today is not just his patience but that he could develop his ideas on his own. In the early twentieth century, most scientists taught in universities. That Einstein maintained his scientific interests while employed in a patent office has made many wonder what fueled his passion.* At the core of this rebellious genius was his nonconformity, his questioning of accepted truths, and his strength to stand by what he believed even when others considered him a failure.

By now we're familiar with the *hook* and the *thesis*. We can tell how they work, how the hook captures out attention with vivid details and the thesis sets out the plan for the essay. But the *context* is much subtler. Let's examine what it does.

Context Checklist:
1. Expands the information given in the hook:
He is patient. He had a remarkable character. He worked in a patent office.

2. Connects the hook with a larger idea:
He could work on his own and not lose his passion.

3. Places us in the historical time, that is, the historical *context*:
This places us in the early twentieth century.

4. Contrasts information with something different to show why it is interesting:
Shows the difference between Einstein and most scientists of that time.

5. Set up the thesis by highlighting the important elements:
He maintained his interest and had passion.

6. Prepare thesis by suggesting a question:
Many wondered at how he fueled his passion.

Do you see how all these work together? They can easily be boiled down into 2-4 sentences. The fact that Einstein is patient and did things differently leads the reader to ask how he managed to be so different and not lose his passion. It all fits together and makes both the thesis and the hook more powerful and important.

Mastering the Context

Practice 1 : Context Worksheets 1-3

On the next three pages are three pairs of hooks and theses. You have already seen them many times, but now you are going to write a context for each pair. Do to so, follow the instructions below.

    1. First reread the paired hook and context.
    2. Find a few elements from the context checklist to write on each line.
    3. If you get stuck, look at the context checklists above.
    4. After you've filled in all of the lines, write a full introductory paragraph.
    5. Try to condense the context lines into 2-4 sentences.

Practice 2: Writing a Context for your own Hook and Thesis

Now take the hook and thesis that you wrote for your historical figure. You are going to do the same exercise that you have just done with context worksheets 1-3. This time you will write them out yourself. Take your time and look at this not as busy work but as a means of developing your style. Repetition is the best way to master the stylistics of writing. As you try to write a context for each pair, think about ways to add sparkling details and to make the characters more exciting. Here's a list of things to keep in mind.

    1. Do you use memorable details.
    2. Do you tell us when the events take place.
    3. Do you clearly link the ideas of the hook with the thesis.

Context Worksheet 1

Hook & Thesis 1:
In order to give himself the liberty necessary for creative thought, Einstein based his life on a firm rejection of authority and accepted that others would consider him a failure.

1. Expands the information given in the hook:

2. Connects the hook with a larger idea:

3. Places us in the historical time, that is, the historical *context*:

4. Contrasts information with something different to show why it is interesting:

5. Set up the thesis by highlighting the important elements:

6. Prepare thesis by suggesting a question:

Einstein's belief that creativity cannot exist without a questioning of authority can be clearly seen during his high school and university studies, the time he spent working as a patent clerk, and even his years as world-famous celebrity.

Context Worksheet 2

Hook & Thesis 2:
At the age of sixteen, the same year that Einstein dropped out of high school and failed the entrance examination to the Swiss Federal Institute of Technology, he also performed the famous thought experiment in which he visualized traveling alongside a beam of light.

1. Expands the information given in the hook:

2. Connects the hook with a larger idea:

3. Places us in the historical time, that is, the historical *context*:

4. Contrasts information with something different to show why it is interesting:

5. Set up the thesis by highlighting the important elements:

6. Prepare thesis by suggesting a question:

Though many of Einstein's greatest achievements took years to receive recognition, the source of his genius could already be seen in his youthful rebelliousness, his courage to take risks and his powerful imagination.

Context Worksheet 3

Hook & Thesis 3:
Though many considered Einstein's years working in the Swiss Patent Office to be a waste of his talent, he later claimed that the job gave him the creative space and even the inspiration for many of the ideas that he would later develop.

1. Expands the information given in the hook:

2. Connects the hook with a larger idea:

3. Places us in the historical time, that is, the historical *context*:

4. Contrasts information with something different to show why it is interesting:

5. Set up the thesis by highlighting the important elements:

6. Prepare thesis by suggesting a question:

Though Einstein studied traditional physics, his genius grew from what others considered to be his failures: his problems in school, his inability to find a teaching position and his job as a patent clerk.

The Persuasive Essay

Persuasion is perhaps one of the greatest skills to have. Often in life, we want others to see things the way we do. We argue with them, and sometimes we even insult them if they don't agree. But a truly persuasive person doesn't need to raise his voice or to insult anyone. He appeals to our sense of reason. He quickly identifies what we believe is right and wrong, and he appeals to those moral values. Through stories, examples and reasoning, he makes us not just hear but *understand* his point of view. This is the purpose of the persuasive essay.

The *persuasive essay* uses logic and reasoning to convince the readers. It shows that one viewpoint or way of reading a book is more legitimate than another. In order to convince its reader, it always uses sequential reasoning and solid evidence in the form of examples and quotations.

Sequential Reasoning:

What is sequential reasoning? It is when you show how you developed your ideas. Some people just make sweeping statements. We have no idea how they came up with their opinions. With sequential reasoning, you show step by step how you came up with your ideas. If you can't find the sequence of your ideas, then your argument will be much easier for someone else to disprove. The most *persuasive* people are those who can take others through an intellectual process step by step and not just tell them what the conclusion is, but show it to them and make them feel that they themselves can come to the same conclusion on their own.

Practice: Sequencing

Write down three things that you believe firmly. Now write down why? Is there a sequence or is it simple? For instance, if you wrote, "Lying is wrong," was it because, "Lying is dishonest." That is called circular logic. It doesn't actually say why lying is wrong. It just repeats itself in different terms.

    1. Try to find at least three steps for each belief you wrote down.
        a. Lying often has the intention of hiding something.
        b. This creates distance between people.
        c. Lying therefore weakens families and communities.

    2. Find an example for each of your steps.
        a. Tell a time when someone lied to hide something.
        b. Explain how this created distance between people.
        c. Show how this distance weakened the community or family.

    3. Can the opposite of your belief be justified?
If so, under what circumstances can be justified? The best way to persuade someone is to show that there are exceptions to your point of view, but that those exceptions don't change the general rules. For instance, lying can be necessary when facing a bully who wants to copy your homework. But this is not a solution to the bully. The situation still needs to be presented to the teacher. It doesn't mean that lying is the right thing to do in all circumstances.

Two Positions

The persuasive essay should address both positions, the one that it supports and that one that it doesn't support. For this reason, the three/five structure works quite well. Do you recall the *legal* and the *rational* forms of the essay? The first body paragraph supports your argument, the second examines the opposing argument, and the third states why your side of the argument it best. The conclusion then rearticulates the thesis in light of what you have shown and discusses what other points might be considered and what questions might remain.

Another very good version of this essay has three supporting points, and in each paragraph you investigate the point. Here, the paragraph structure is a bit different, because, in each, you state your point, introduce the supporting information, then state the opposing point and disprove it. Then you conclude that point, all in one paragraph. It sounds challenging, but it's actually a very strong and relatively easy form to use.

The Best Way to Win an Argument with Anyone

You steal their argument! For instance, you and a friend are arguing over whether a basketball went out of bounds.

You tell your friend, "I know that you're going to tell me that the ball went out of bounds because it bounced so close to the line. From where you're standing, it could look that way. But actually, because I'm standing closer, I could see the line more clearly than you could, and there is no doubt about where it landed."

All right, the response is a bit formal, but it works. What can your friend respond? "Um, no, I mean, you're right that it looked like it was close to the line but really..."

You've stolen his argument. He has nothing left to say. He can only insist and say, No over and over again (unless he is a very strategic debater).

In all arguments, you want to consider how to neutralize the other person's argument. It's like a joke or a funny remark. Even if everyone is thinking it, the person who says it first gets the credit. So if you state your opponent's argument first, when he tries to use it he's going to sound as if he's copying you. Therefore, you are automatically in the winner's position.

Try this (but not too aggressively) the next time you have an argument.

For instance: "Dad, I know you're going to say that I forgot to clean my room, and *you're right about that*–I did forget to clean it. I'm sorry, but I had a reason. You see, I was..."

In this response, your reason doesn't matter. The other person thinks he has won because you've not only said he's right and that you're sorry, but by the time you've supplied your reason, there's not much he can say. You've actually dismissed his point.

This technique works in many ways, but the essence is that you state your weaknesses immediately. That way the other person can't point out your weaknesses. Someone who always tries to appear strong or who tries to have a flawless argument is open for attack. Everyone knows that all people have weaknesses and that all arguments have flaws.

"Okay, so I'm not the most persuasive person in the world, certainly not as persuasive as you are, but in this case, I think I may have a point..."

Persuasive Writing in American Culture

Perhaps the most famous example of persuasive writing present in American culture is the State of the Union address given annually by the President of the United States. This address is written to convince the citizens not only that the President's plan will be beneficial to the United States, but also to convince the public of the country's current and continued success.

Practice: Persuasive Writing in Everyday Life

Go home and look around the house. See if you can find examples of persuasive writing. Look at magazines and newspapers in particular. Are they trying to persuade you of anything? Are ads a form of persuasion? How about articles about eating healthy foods? Are articles about politics always objective, or do they sometimes try to persuade? Find two examples of persuasive writing that you can bring to class.

Number each article and explain below why it is persuasive.

1.

2.

Now explain what you would have to change for it to be expository.

1.

2.

The Persuasive Thesis

The persuasive thesis is different from the expository thesis insofar as it clearly takes one position as opposed to another. Implicit in a persuasive thesis a sense of something that should happen and something else that should not, or of one position that would be better, more successful or preferable to another.

For example, an expository thesis might read as follows:

According to Cherokee tradition, Two Crows is supposed to die because Blue Jay's spirit must be set free, because of the need to keep peace and harmony, and because the consequences of not following tradition may be severe.

While this thesis explains *why* something is done, it is far too matter of fact to be a persuasive thesis. It doesn't say whether Two Crows should live or die. It only says that *according to Cherokee tradition* he is supposed to die. Then it lists the reasons. Its tone is objective, and, by reading it, we expect to learn about Cherokee tradition, not whether one argument is better than another.

What would be the persuasive thesis? Read the checklist on the next page, and write an answer to each of the lines. Then return to this page and try to write a persuasive thesis here:

Re-evaluate your thesis after reading these question:

- Do you have a clear sense of what it proves?

- Do you know what it will disprove?

- Can you support it with concrete evidence that aren't general "truths"?

- Does the thesis suggest the main elements of its structure (checklist #5)?

Try rewriting your thesis again, differently this time, and see in what ways you can make it stronger.

Practice: Write two more persuasive theses using the checklist. Take arguments that you might not usually consider and see if you can support them. *Don't forget to list the three main elements of your thesis in order of importance, from least to most.*

Persuasive Thesis Checklist

1. Choose your position. Which side of the issue do you support, and what solution will you offer? Should he die? Or should he live? If you don't know this and you can't say why, then you don't know the purpose of your essay.

2. Have you chosen your side because of gut impulse or because you have thought the problem through. Be careful when using "truths." For instance, people say, "Killing is wrong." Is that a hard fact, or is that a general truth? Make sure your argument has actual evidence, then try to write a sequence explaining how you came to hold your position. If you can't do this yet, go to #3.

3. Research your topic. How much supporting material do you have? A persuasive essay must provide specific and convincing evidence. Do you have the resources necessary? By researching and reading, can you support the logical sequence that explains why you chose your side of the argument?

4. Consider what the other argument might be. Try to prove yourself wrong. Try to find a logical sequence for the other side.

5. Structure your essay. Choose one of the two approaches. Make sure that you can explain the main points of your essay in one sentence.

Here is one approach:
In the first, you support your view (offering all of your main points).
In the second, you explain the opposing argument (discredit detracting points).
In the third, you show why your argument is superior.

Here is a second approach:
Choose three points that support your argument. In each paragraph you analyze one of them and at the same time discredit the opposing argument. Pick your three points.

A Thesis in Two Sentences?

Usually, the thesis is in one sentence, but sometimes the organizing details are in the sentence that follows. In this way, the thesis can appear to be in two sentences. This is perfectly normal and often allows for a strong, clear and more dramatic thesis since you will then give the rest of the information in the following sentence.

However, an *expository* thesis works much better in one sentence since it is designed to teach, and the three elements are difficult to separate from the thesis. This isn't always the case. On the other hand, a *persuasive* thesis works particularly well in two sentences.

For instance, let's consider the expository thesis we've already studied:

According to Cherokee tradition, Two Crows is supposed to die because Blue Jay's spirit must be set free, because of the need to keep peace and harmony, and because the consequences of not following tradition may be severe.

Now let's turn it into a rather simple persuasive thesis:

Two Crows should die because Blue Jay's spirit must be set free, because of the need to keep peace and harmony, and because the consequences of not following tradition may be severe.

Now let's rewrite it as two sentences. The first will be a more complex thesis while the second gives the order in which we will examine the thesis.

Not only to appease Cherokee tradition but to promote the safety of his tribe, Two Crows should die. Though the reasons for this might not seem substantial in our terms, in the world of the Cherokee, the death is absolutely necessary to set free Blue Jay's spirit, to keep peace and harmony, and to prevent the other severe consequences that can result from not following tradition.

Do you see how much stronger the thesis sounds now? By using two sentences, we are able to lead into the thesis in the first and state our position clearly. In the second, we reiterate and support the thesis and give the three main points that we will learn about in the essay.

Practice 1: Reread the theses on this page. Highlight and number the three points.

Practice 2: Take the persuasive thesis sentences you have written up to this point and rewrite them in two sentences. Make sure that the thesis is clearly stated in the first and that the second explains how you will examine it and gives your three main points.

Introduction Guide

- Hook: should hook your reader in, catch his attention and be stylistically exciting.
  - Historical information
  - Surprising statement
  - Character sketch
  - Anecdote
  - Declaration

- Context: should bridge the hook and the thesis and set up the main ideas.
  - Expands information in the hook
  - Connects the hook with a larger idea
  - Gives the historical timeframe
  - Contrasts the hook information to show why it is interesting
  - Set up the thesis by highlighting the important elements
  - Prepare thesis by suggesting (not asking) a question

- Thesis: should assert main point, suggest evidence and structure the argument.
  - Tells what you will teach (for expository)
  - (Or) Tells what you will prove (for persuasive)
  - Gives the three main elements of your essay (in order of importance)

Writing the Body Paragraphs: From the Thesis to the Body

The three main essay paragraphs (or the body of the essay) are where you show whether or not the ideas of your introduction have any substance. But often times, students write through an essay without any sense of beginning or end. Perhaps you have a clear sense of introduction, but once you are into the body of the essay, how do you know how to organize your discussion? Essays can easily become a jumble of details that the reader struggles to sort through.

How do you avoid this?

It's simple.

Imagine that each of the three body paragraphs is a mini essay.

Wait! You're probably thinking, 'Oh no, I sat down having to write one essay, but now I have to write three more…'

That's not how it works. This will make essay writing much easier.

To begin with, if you're writing a 3/5 essay, how do you know what the body paragraphs will discuss. It's simple mathematics. Your thesis has three main points. In your thesis, they should be listed from least to most important.

Let's write a thesis about how Rain Dove matures. This is a *literary* thesis, but it's not necessarily a persuasive thesis unless you really feel that you need to prove a point. Otherwise, the form would resemble an expository thesis.

To build our thesis, we look at the assignment. *Rain Dove matures or evolves.* That's going to be a clue. You can say this many ways, but we'll keep it simple since you'll be writing this paper and coming up with fancier ways to say all this.

Now let's look at the list of elements. Pick at least three that describe how she evolves.

- Her ability to trust herself?
- Her sense of inner strength and courage?
- How she thinks about community?
- Her role as a mother?
- Her role as a woman within Cherokee society?
- Her ability to push or blur the traditional gender boundaries?
- Her outlook on life and its cyclical nature?
- Her understanding of the Cherokee concepts of balance and harmony?

Here's the beginning of a rough thesis that isn't very fancy:

Rain Dove evolves in several ways: in her ability to trust herself, in her sense of inner strength and courage, and in how she thinks about her community.

This is a very simple thesis. When writing yours, try to find your own voice. Don't forget to revise the earlier lessons on the thesis.

Now for the simple mathematics.

What are the three main points of the thesis? (We'll be repetitive so you get the point.)

1 • How Rain Dove evolves in her ability to trust herself.

2 • How she evolves in her sense of inner strength and courage.

3 • How she evolves in the way that she thinks about her community.

Now you have the three main body paragraphs. There's no magic involved. In your thesis, you should list the three main points in the order that you will discuss them in the body. Each body paragraph will work towards proving your thesis.

Now let's look at the basic structure of a body paragraph, in this case the first.

- **Topic Sentence:** introduces the first main idea while suggesting the thesis.
- **Argument:** tells us what you think in detail.
- **Example:** supports what you think.
- **Analysis of example:** ties back to argument and carries your ideas forward.
- **Transition:** concludes analysis of first main point, refers back to thesis, and readies readers for the second main point.

Now let's fit the information into the form (go to the next page).

Body Paragraph Guide

Take point 1: How Rain Dove evolves in her ability to trust herself.

- **Topic Sentence** (this is a simple version):
Rain Dove evolves in her ability to trust herself.

- **Argument:**
Give a sense of her character. How much did she trust herself before. What events caused her to have more trust. How much change does she experience.

- **Example:**
Give an example of this change. Find a quotation from the text that shows how she changed and why.

- **Analysis of example:**
Look at what you wrote in the argument section. Now explain how the example that you just gave contributes to your argument.

- **Transition:**
Conclude your analysis by summing up (not repeating) the importance of Rain Dove's growth. In doing so, make sure that you remind us of the thesis. Without telling exactly what the next topic sentence is going to be, try to suggest the transition.

For instance: *Through these life-changing events* (be specific and name them), *Rain Dove not only learns to trust herself but begins to understand what it means to be strong.*

The word "strong" prepares the reader for the next topic sentence which will deal with how Rain Dove develops a sense of inner strength and courage. You can then, in the next topic sentence, explain this more clearly and go through the same mini-essay process again.

Practice:
Using the essay structure above, write this body paragraph. Find examples from the text.

NOTE: Remind yourself often of the thesis:
Let's look at the thesis again. Have we wandered from it? Has the first paragraph answered the first part of the thesis. Has it readied us for the next part.

Rain Dove evolves in several ways: in her ability to trust herself, in her sense of inner strength and courage, and in how she thinks about her community.

Preparing your own essay

It's your turn to write a thesis statement.

First pick three ways that you think Rain Dove evolved.

On a separate sheet of paper, write a few versions of the same thesis statement. Experiment with language and see how different you can make them even though you are saying the same thing. Make sure you list the three main points of thesis in order of importance.

Write your thesis here:

Now let's think about turning it into an essay. Number the three points. Imagine how they fit together. Do they give a sense of the growing importance of the subject matter as well as the "narrative continuity."

Narrative Continuity:
The term sounds pretty fancy, but once again the idea is simple. Narrative continuity is when the narrative (the story) is told in a continuous fashion. For example, a literary analysis could simply examine three different uses of a symbol in a novel. But naturally it would make the most sense to organize the discussion as progressively as possible. This isn't always possible, but often symbols and themes evolve progressively with the characters, so it's actually quite natural to tell the story in a continuous fashion.

Practice 1:
Write your three main points below. Then write a few events beneath each that corresponds with them. See if you can give a sense of the story in the order it was told. While your examples don't have to be in perfect order, it helps if you can show how the story develops through your analysis.

Main Point 1:

Main Point 2:

Main Point 3:

Practice 2:
Look at the three *body paragraph worksheets*. They are almost identical. Take a highlighter and a read through them. Try to see what changes in each of the three worksheets. At the bottom of each worksheet write what it does that the others don't do.

Practice 3:
Using your three main points and the novel for material, fill in the worksheets. Then use the worksheets to help you write the paragraphs.

Body Paragraph 1 Worksheet

Your Thesis:

The first main point of you thesis:

    – Body Paragraph 1 Begins –
Transform main point 1 into a topic sentence:

Explain this topic sentence, providing a reasonable argument:

(Include where this fits in the narrative continuity.)

Find a solid example that supports your argument:

Analyze your example and tie it back to your argument:

Conclude paragraph and transition to main point 2:

_____

    Question: What does this paragraph do that the others don't do?

Body Paragraph 2 Worksheet

Your Thesis (you should keep your thesis within sight at all times while writing):

The second main point of you thesis:

–Body Paragraph 2 Begins–
Transform main point 2 into a topic sentence:

Explain this topic sentence, providing a reasonable argument (don't repeat your argument from paragraph 1, but try to build on the previous argument):

(Don't forget the narrative continuity. It will help you order your argument.)

Find a solid example that supports your argument:

Analyze your example and tie it back to your argument:

Conclude paragraph, refer back to main point 1, and transition to main point 3:

_____

Question: What does this paragraph do that the others don't do?

Body Paragraph 3 Worksheet

Your Thesis (yes, write it out again):

The third main point of you thesis:

– Body Paragraph 3 Begins –
Transform main point 3 into a topic sentence:

Explain this topic sentence, providing a reasonable argument that builds off of the arguments in paragraphs 1 & 2:

(Narrative continuity is more important. Give us a sense of process and change.)

Find a solid example that supports your argument:

Analyze your example and tie it back to your argument:

Conclude paragraph, refer back to main points 1 & 2, transition to conclusion:

_____

Question: What does this paragraph do that the others don't do?

Mastering the Topic Sentence

What does it do?
1. Expresses the main idea of a paragraph.
2. Refers back to one of the main points of the thesis.
3. Tells the reader what to expect in the information that will follow.
4. Limits the subject matter that you will discuss with a controlling idea.
5. Summarizes your approach to the subject matter.

The topic sentence is like a mini-thesis the way that a paragraph is like a mini-essay.

Topic sentences have both a topic and a controlling idea. The topic refers back to your thesis, and the controlling idea tells us how you will examine that part of the thesis.

For instance:
Many historians forgive Columbus's involvement in the slave trade because, according to them, <u>it was considered acceptable by his culture.</u>

The first half of the sentence is the topic (Columbus's involvement in the slave trade), and the underlined part is the controlling idea (how it was seen by his culture).

Let's imagine that in your thesis, you are going to persuade us that Columbus was not a villain despite three actions most people usually associate with villainy: slavery, robbery and killing. These will be the three main points and therefore the three topics for the main paragraphs. But each topic then needs a controlling idea which will tell *how* you plan on examining the topic.

The controlling idea can also be consider the *Why?* As in, *why* is this main topic important.

Let's break the sentence up to understand this better. Turn to the next page.

Practice: Topic Sentences

First try to find the controlling ideas for the topic sentences 2 and 3. Are they the same as topic sentence 1? Can you find other controlling ideas that might explain *how* you'll prove that he's not a villain for this particular crime?

Imaginary Essay One: Columbus is Innocent

Topic Sentence 1
Topic (main point 1): not a villain because of the slave trade

Controlling idea: acceptable to his culture.

Topic Sentence 2
Topic (main point 2): not a villain because of robbery

Controlling idea: *why?*

Topic Sentence 3
Topic (main point 3): not a villain because of killing

Controlling idea: *why?*

Switch the Perspective:
Now do the same exercise for all three topic sentences, but this time find reasons *why* Columbus is guilty for each of these particular actions.

Imaginary Essay Two: Columbus is Guilty

Topic Sentence 1
Topic (main point 1): a villain because of the slave trade

Controlling idea:

Topic Sentence 2
Topic (main point 2): a villain because of robbery

Controlling idea:

Topic Sentence 3
Topic (main point 3): a villain because of killing

Controlling idea:

Steps Towards Writing Your *Persuasive* Columbus Essay

1. Ask yourself whether you think Columbus is a criminal.

Yes   *or...*   No

2. Investigate your answer. Don't rely on "truths" or gut feelings. Find concrete reasons. List your reasons here:

3. Make a sequence of at least three steps that shows how you came to your decision.
   1.

   2.

   3.

4. Now find three main points that will support what you believe.
   1.

   2.

   3.

5. Turn this into your thesis. This is a *persuasive* thesis. Use one or two sentences.

6. Reread your thesis and make sure that the three main points are in order of importance. Readjust if necessary:

7. Ask yourself whether "narrative continuity" can apply to your thesis. Reorder if necessary:

8. Go to the next page…

9. Structuring your essay

Rewrite your thesis here (remember to look back at your thesis when writing):

Separate your three main points into the three topics:

Topic Sentence 1
Topic (main point 1): Villain or explorer because of… *A*

Controlling idea: *A* is villainous or not because of…
1.
2.
3.
4.

Topic Sentence 2
Topic (main point 2): Villain or explorer because of… **B**

Controlling idea: *B* is villainous or not because of…
1.
2.
3.
4.

Topic Sentence 3
Topic (main point 3): Villain or explorer because of… **C**

Controlling idea: *C* is villainous or not because of…
1.
2.
3.
4.

The "controlling idea" areas are still blank.
Brainstorm as many possible reasons *why* he is villainous or not.
Now, pick the best controlling idea for each (you can pick more than one if they fit).
Write your three topic sentences:
Topic Sentence 1:

Topic Sentence 2:

Topic Sentence 3:

Verifying your Topic Sentences with the Checklist

Rewrite your thesis and your three topic sentences:

Thesis:

Topic Sentence 1:

Topic Sentence 2:

Topic Sentence 3:

For each topic sentence, read through the checklist:
1. Expresses the main idea of a paragraph.
2. Refers back to one of the main points of the thesis.
3. Tells the reader what to expect in the information that will follow.
4. Limits the subject matter that you will discuss with a controlling idea.
5. Summarizes your approach to the subject matter.

Making your topic sentence stronger # 1

- Use words that suggest growing importance or process.
- For instance, for topic sentence 3, you can use *finally* or words that suggest culmination or intensifying.

Practice:
Rewrite your topic sentences using sequence words.

Topic Sentence 1:

Topic Sentence 2:

Topic Sentence 3:

Making your topic sentence stronger # 2

For topic sentences 2 and 3, see if you can hint back to your previous paragraph and help connect the themes. This way, when you read the topic sentence, you understand how it fits with the previous topic.

For instance, re-read the following topic sentence:
Many historians forgive Columbus's involvement in the slave trade because, according to them, it was considered acceptable by his culture.

Now imagine that it were the second topic sentence:
Though slavery is more difficult to justify than material theft, many historians forgive Columbus' involvement in the slave trade because, according to them, it was considered acceptable by his culture.

Now imagine that it were the third topic sentence:
Of all his perceived wrong-doings, Columbus's involvement in the slave trade is that which historians forgive because, according to them, it was considered acceptable by his culture.

Practice 1:
Using a highlighter, mark the differences in the second and third versions of the topic sentence.

Now explain why each is different and how it would reinforce to the order of the essay.

Version 2:

Version 3:

Practice 2:
Do the same exercise for each of your topic sentences. Adapt each one so that we know if it is first, second or third. For the first, try to use a sequence word. Remember that sequence words can be used in each of the three.

Topic Sentence 1:

Topic Sentence 2:

Topic Sentence 3:

Expository Refresher

By now, we're familiar with the expository essay. We know that its job is to explain, and that it originally comes from the Latin word expositor, which means "one who exposes."

Here are some rules:

• The thesis of an expository essay should tell us a general topic as well as three things that we are going to learn about that topic. Your job is to identify a general theme or topic in a subject matter, and then to expose three aspects of that theme.

• The three aspects of that theme should be listed in order of importance, starting with the least important and progressing to the most. The list can also be given chronologically in terms of years or process (for instance, explaining how a situation developed).

Building the essay:

This time we're going to let you do your own thesis. You've already mastered that skill.

Then we're going to walk you through the writing of an expository essay in which you will use da Vinci's life to develop the definition of a Renaissance man.

Here are the main steps of development:

1 • Write thesis statement with thee main points.
2 • Separate three main points into body paragraph subjects.
3 • Turn each main point into a topic sentence.
4 • Find the controlling idea for each topic sentence.
5 • Give the topic sentences a sense of sequence or progression.

We already know that your thesis will somehow deal with the definition of Renaissance man. There are dozens of ways to explore this question. Your main points could involve da Vinci's general philosophy, or you could simply discuss the major aspects of his work.

Now, on the *Renaissance Man Essay Worksheet*, go through all five of the steps above.

After you've finished the worksheet, you will go on to the next page and use the information that you've generated to write your own *transitions*.

Renaissance Man Essay Worksheet

1. Thesis with three main points:

2. Body paragraph main points:

    BP1:

    BP2:

    BP3:

3. Simple topic sentences:

    TS1:

    TS2:

    TS3:

4. Complex topic sentences (with controlling idea):

    TS1:

    TS2:

    TS3:

5. Rewrite topic sentences to give a sense of sequence or progression:

    TS1:

    TS2:

    TS3:

What is a Transition?

transition, n.
1. movement, passage, or change from one position, state, stage, subject, concept, etc., to another; change: the transition from adolescence to adulthood.
2. a passage from one scene to another by sound effects, music, etc., as in a television program, theatrical production, or the like.
3. to make a transition: He had difficulty transitioning from enlisted man to officer.
[1545–55; < L tr nsiti n- a going across, equiv. to tr nsit(us) (trans re to cross]

The *transition* helps the reader cross from one paragraph to the next, from one main point to the subject that follows.

For now, let's imagine that two of the three main points are *science* and *art*. You've just finished paragraph 1 which is about science, and you want to transition to paragraph 2 which is about art.

Here's the last two lines of paragraph 1:

Though science was clearly foundational in da Vinci's vision of the world, it in no way detracted from his artistic ambitions. In fact, for him, art found its harmony in a scientific understanding of the world.

Do you see how this sentence prepares us for paragraph 2, which will be about art. The *transition* in paragraph 1 gradually shifted the focus from science to the relationship of science and art. The reader immediately understands that the next paragraph will focus on art. In fact, the topic sentence of the following paragraph can also have an element of transition. We've already touched on this in our discussion of sequence and process. That's part of a transition. Look at the sheet titled *Transition Words*, and you will see how natural a transition is.

Now here's the same ending to paragraph 1, but this time followed by the transitional topic sentence of paragraph 2.

Though science was clearly foundational in da Vinci's vision of the world, it in no way detracted from his artistic ambitions. In fact, for him, art found its harmony in a scientific understanding of the world.
    Unquestionably, as with science, art was essential for the Renaissance man.

Do you see how *unquestionably* and *as with science* both help transition.
- *Unquestionably* helps make a clear shift into the next paragraph.
- *As with science* refers back to the previous question.

Also, a transition should help conclude the subject matter of its paragraph. The transition above does so by stating the foundational importance of science.

Now go to the *Mastering Transitions* sheet.

Transition Words

To Add: again, and then, besides, equally important, finally, further, furthermore, nor, too, next, lastly, what's more, moreover, in addition, first (second, etc.), indeed, in fact

To Compare: whereas, yet, on the other hand, however, nevertheless, on the other hand, on the contrary, by comparison, where, compared to, up against, balanced against, vis a vis, but, although, conversely, meanwhile, after all, in contrast, although this may be true

To Prove: because, for, since, for the same reason, obviously, evidently, furthermore, moreover, besides, indeed, in fact, in addition, in any case, that is

To Show Exception: yet, still, however, nevertheless, in spite of, despite, of course, once in a while, sometimes

To Show Time: immediately, thereafter, soon, after a few hours, finally, then, later, previously, formerly, first (second, etc.), next, and then

To Repeat: in brief, as I have said, as I have noted, as has been noted,

To Emphasize: definitely, extremely, obviously, in fact, indeed, in any case, absolutely, positively, naturally, surprisingly, always, forever, perennially, eternally, never, emphatically, unquestionably, without a doubt, certainly, undeniably, without reservation

To Show Sequence: first, second, third, and so forth. A, B, C, and so forth. next, then, following this, at this time, now, at this point, after, afterward, subsequently, finally, consequently, previously, before this, simultaneously, concurrently, thus, therefore, hence, next, and then, soon

To Indicate a Cause or Reason: as, because of, due to, for, for the reason that, since

To Indicate a Purpose or Reason Why: for fear that, in the hope that, in order to, so, so that, with this in mind

To Indicate a Result or an Effect: accordingly, finally, consequently, hence, so, therefore, thus

To Give an Example: for example, for instance, in this case, in another case, on this occasion, in this situation, take the case of, to demonstrate, to illustrate, as an illustration, to illustrate, in particular, particularly, specifically

To Summarize or Conclude:
in brief, on the whole, summing up, to conclude, in conclusion, as I have shown, as I have said, hence, therefore, accordingly, thus, as a result, consequently, on the whole,

Mastering Transitions

Now take your *Renaissance Man Essay Worksheet* and copy the three topic sentences:

TS1:

TS2:

TS3:

Can you add any words from the *transition words* page?

Using the transition below as an example, write a transition to the paragraph preceding your topic sentence.

Though science was clearly foundational in da Vinci's vision of the world, it in no way detracted from his artistic ambitions. In fact, for him, art found its harmony in a scientific understanding of the world.
     Unquestionably, as with science, art was essential for the Renaissance man.

Remember to look at the lists of transition words.

Transition 1 from paragraph 1 to TS 2: (write TS2 on the line just below)

Transition 1 from paragraph 1 to TS 2: (write TS2 on the line just below)

Now ask yourself these questions:
      1 • Does the transition sentence suggest the topic sentence of the next paragraph?
      2 • Do you make a clear break between the transition and the topic sentence?
      3 • Does the topic sentence refer back to the transition sentence?
      4 • Do you use transition words to emphasize the change of subject matter?
      5 • Does the transition sentence conclude the subject matter in its paragraph?

How to Conclude (the thesis affirmed but not repeated)

The conclusion is the most misunderstood part of the essay. Often, students think that they should simply repeat their introduction, but this is not the case at all. Rather, the conclusion should restate an affirmed and redeveloped thesis, then proceed to reflect upon the material discussed, address loose ends and other aspects that might deserve further development.

Take a look at the definition.

> **conclusion**, n.
> 1. the end or close; final part.
> 2. the last main division of a discourse, usually containing a summing up of the points and a statement of opinion or decisions reached.
> 3. a result, issue, or outcome; settlement or arrangement: The restitution payment was one of the conclusions of the negotiations.
> 4. final decision: The judge has reached his conclusion.
> 5. a reasoned deduction or inference.
> (from Dictionary.com)

Nowhere in this definition do we see the word "repeat." The closest we come to that is "summing up." But to sum up is quite a different act. When you sum up an argument, you show how a thesis has been transformed by the information provided in the body paragraphs.

For example, imagine that you go to the cinema. You are watching a movie about Joe, a young man who moves to New York City so that he can pursue his dream of being a musician. He meets a girl, Kate, and he falls in love. But Kate tells him that she doesn't trust anyone, much less men or musicians. He says he's a good man and that he'll prove it to her.

This is the movie's introduction. We know the context, and we know that the movie is going to show us whether Joe is a good man or not (the thesis). But shortly after Joe says this, a murder is committed at the music club where is plays. He has to prove his innocence, and no one believes him. But finally, after an hour of adventure, he proves that he's really innocent. Kate says to him, "Joe, you really are a good and kind man, and I don't know how I could have been so wrong." This is the conclusion. They live happily ever after, or at least that's how it seems when the movie ends. Is it a good movie? Probably not, but it does have a thesis and a conclusion. Though the thesis and the conclusion resemble each other, they are not the same. The thesis is trying to show something, but the conclusion is reflecting on what has been shown. Imagine that the movie ended with Joe saying, "I'm a good man, and I'll prove it." That would be a repetition of the thesis, and we'd all think, "Why did I just sit through this terrible romance if I'm back to the introduction?"

Let's practice the first step of writing a good conclusion. The *affirmed thesis*.

The Affirmed Thesis

The *affirmed thesis* is often the first line of the conclusion, and it both sums up the argument as well as affirms it. (Note that the three main points are often not present in the affirmed thesis.)

Look at these examples:

–1–
Thesis: Though unfairly accused of having eaten the candy, I am in truth innocent because not only do I dislike candy but I am allergic to sugar and I am terrified of cavities.

Affirmed thesis: Without a doubt, someone who loathes candy, is allergic to it and suffers from a terror of cavities should not be accused of having eaten it but rather should be praised for his self-control in a society crippled by sugar addiction.

–2–
Thesis: Though Einstein studied traditional physics, his genius grew from what others considered to be his failures: his problems in school, his inability to find a teaching position and his job as a patent clerk.

Affirmed thesis: Even if Einstein's studies were to some degree important for his intellectual development, unquestionably it was his problems, failures and unorthodox approaches to his career that not only set him apart but gave him the space to let his genius flourish.

– 3 –
Thesis: Two Crows should die because Blue Jay's spirit must be set free, because of the need to keep peace and harmony, and because the consequences of not following tradition may be severe.

Affirmed thesis: In consideration of the grave consequences that Two Crows' tribe would suffer if he were to live, he should die and trust that both Blue Jay's spirit as well as his own people will find the peace and harmony that is so difficult to maintain.

Practice:
Number 1-4 on a sheet, and explain how each affirmed thesis develops the original thesis and concludes it. Also write down suggestions that you think might result in a stronger affirmed thesis. Then take two theses from your previous essays and affirm them.

Continuation of the Hook

A conclusion can start with two elements:
1 • The affirmed thesis, or
2 • A continuation of the hook building on the opening hook and context.

The continuation of the hook is meant to resituate what we've learned in the body paragraphs by reintroducing information from the introduction. Imagine that the introduction is the beginning of a story; the continuation of the hook finishes the story.

If the conclusion begins with the continuation of the hook, then the second sentence should be the affirmed thesis. The two can also work together.

Example of the continuation of the hook:

Original hook: Though many considered Einstein's years working in the Swiss Patent Office to be a waste of his talent, he later claimed that the job gave him the creative space and even the inspiration for many of the ideas that he would later develop.

Thesis: Though Einstein studied traditional physics, his genius grew from what others considered to be his failures: his problems in school, his inability to find a teaching position and his job as a patent clerk.

Continuation of the hook: Though Einstein could have avoided mentioning his job in the Swiss Patent Office, the fact that he often discussed it in relation to his work suggests just how important it was.

Affirmed thesis: Even if Einstein's studies were important for his intellectual development, unquestionably it was his problems, failures and unorthodox approaches to his career that not only set him apart but gave him the space to let his genius flourish.

Now read the last two together (with a transition word to connect them):
Though Einstein could have avoided mentioning his job in the Swiss Patent Office, the fact that he often discussed it in relation to his work suggests just how important it was. Consequently, even if his studies were important for his intellectual development, unquestionably it was his problems, failures and unorthodox approaches to his career that not only set him apart but gave him the space to let his genius flourish.

Practice:
Look back on your previous essays. Choose a hook and thesis from one of them. Now rewrite both with a continuation and an affirmation. Use the paragraph above as a model.

Mastering the Conclusion

Here are the steps to writing a good conclusion:

1 • If your essay needs to be resituated, then write a continuation of your hook.
2 • Take your thesis and transform it into an affirmation.
3 • Write a sentence or two summarizing evidence or events.
4 • Shift thesis from the framework of your discussion to a larger picture.
      To do so, ask yourself these questions and write the answers:

• What is the significance of your findings?
• What are the implications of the conclusion for this topic and the broader field?
• Are there any limitations to your approach?
• Are there any points of relevance that influence the topic but fell outside the scope of the essay?
• Are there any suggestions you can make in terms of future research?
• What questions can you end with to suggest the implications of your essay?

Here are a few things that you shouldn't do in a conclusion:

• Don't assume that the reader has fully grasped your point already. The essay isn't over.
• Don't simply restate what you've said in the introduction and body paragraphs.
• Don't make claims in your conclusion that you haven't supported in your essay.
• Don't introduce information that will alter the analysis made in your essay.

Conclusion Worksheet

Hook (from introduction):

Thesis:

1. Continuation of hook:

2. Affirmed thesis:

3. Summarize evidence or events:

4. Shift thesis from the framework of your discussion to a larger picture.
       Answer these questions:

- **What is the significance of your findings?**

- **What are the implications of the conclusion for this topic and the broader field?**

- **Are there any limitations to your approach?**

- **Are there any points of relevance that influence the topic but fell outside the scope of the essay?**

- **Are there any suggestions you can make in terms of future research?**

- **What questions can you end with to suggest the implications of your essay?**

Introduction Refresher

Answer the following questions:

1 • What are the three main parts of an introduction?

2 • When preparing an introduction, with what part do you begin?

3 • When writing an introduction, with what part do you begin?

In the sections below, explain the three key concepts as if you were going to have to teach them.

Concept 1: _____

Concept 2: _____

Concept 3: _____

Now write one of each for your persuasive letter to King George.

Concept 1: _____

Concept 2: _____

Concept 3: _____

Body Paragraph Refresher

After reading the information below, can you create an instruction sheet for each body paragraph?

Each body paragraph follows a basic shift from general to specific to general again. Remember that general does not mean vague.

- General idea
- Analysis that becomes more specific
- Example
- Analysis of specifics
- Synthesis (general again)
- Conclusion and transition

If this were the basic plan, how would you translate it into concrete terms? Look back at the information on the body paragraph that you received in class.

Write out the new model below:

On a separate page, outline your letter to King George based on this model:

Conclusion Refresher

Answer the following questions:

1. What is the most important part of a conclusion?

2. What are two types of beginnings for a conclusion?
    1.

    2.

3. What do you use to resituate the conclusion in its context?

4. What do you summarize in the conclusion?
(Is there more than one answer to this question?)

5. List two things you should never do in a conclusion.
    1.

    2.

6. List three questions that your conclusion should try to answer.
    1.

    2.

    3.

7. What is a good way to end a conclusion?

Concluding the Letter to King George

Now plan the conclusion of your letter to King George.

1. Does your conclusion need to be resituated in the context?

2. Considering question #1, how will you begin the conclusion?

3. If you have one, what is the continuation of the hook?

4. What is you affirmed thesis:

5. What events and examples will you summarize?

6. Three questions that your conclusion should try to answer.
    1.

    2.

    3.

7. How will you end your conclusion?

Building an Essay Guide

Read back over the essay handouts you've receive and try to write up a guide that lists the main elements in each part of an essay.

Introduction:

Body paragraph 1:

Body paragraph 2:

Body paragraph 3:

Conclusion:

Essay Guide

Introduction:
- Hook: should hook your reader in, catch his attention and be stylistically exciting.
- Context: should bridge the hook and the thesis and set up the main ideas.
- Thesis: should assert main point, suggest evidence and structure the argument.

Body paragraph 1:
- **Topic Sentence with controlling idea:** introduces the first main point while suggesting the thesis. Don't forget to use transition words.
- **Argument:** tells us what you think in detail. Keep in mind *narrative continuity*.
- **Example:** supports what you think.
- **Analysis of example:** ties back to argument and carries your ideas forward.
- **Transition:** concludes analysis of first main point, refers back to thesis, and readies readers for the second main point.

Body paragraph 2:
- **Topic Sentence with controlling idea:** introduces the second main point while reminding us of the thesis and of the first main point if necessary. The second point should continue the narrative, offer a contradictory argument or sequential effect, etc. Don't forget to use transition words.
- **Argument:** tells us what you think in detail. Keep in mind *narrative continuity*.
- **Example:** supports what you think.
- **Analysis of example:** ties back to argument and to body paragraph 1. Carries your ideas forward.
- **Transition:** concludes analysis of first main point, refers back to thesis and to first main point. Readies readers for the third main point.

Body paragraph 3:
- **Topic Sentence with controlling idea:** introduces the third main point while reminding us of the thesis and of the first two main points if necessary. The second point should continue the narrative, offer a contradictory argument or sequential effect, etc. Don't forget to use transition words.
- **Argument:** tells us what you think in detail. Keep in mind *narrative continuity*.
- **Example:** supports what you think.
- **Analysis of example:** ties back to argument and to body paragraphs 1 and 2. Carries your ideas forward.
- **Transition:** concludes analysis of first main point, refers back to thesis and to first and second main points. Readies readers for the third main point.

Conclusion:
- Continuation of the hook only if the conclusion needs to be resituated.
- Affirmed thesis that does not repeat but restates the original thesis.
- Sentence or two summarizing evidence or events.
- Shift thesis from the framework of your discussion to a larger picture.

- What is the significance of your findings?
- What are the implications of the conclusion for this topic and the broader field?
- Are there any limitations to your approach?
- Are there any points of relevance that influence the topic but fell outside the scope of the essay?
- Are there any suggestions you can make in terms of future research?
- What questions can you end with to suggest the implications of your essay?

Made in the USA
Columbia, SC
28 February 2020